Poems Before Easter

Poems Before Easter

BARBARA GLENN

With Foreword by

N. SCOTT MOMADAY

and Introduction by

KENNETH FIELDS

UNIVERSITY OF NEW MEXICO PRESS   ALBUQUERQUE

Library of Congress Cataloging-in-Publication Data

Glenn, Barbara, 1942–

  Poems before Easter / Barbara Glenn.

    p. cm.

  ISBN 978-0-8263-4846-3 (paper : alk. paper)

  I. Title.

  PS3607.L44P64 2011

  811'.6—dc22]

                    2010030558

Text composed in Dante MT Std 10.5/13.5

Design and composition: Melissa Tandysh

Poems by Myriam Diocaretz were previously published in *Que no se pueden decir.*
New York, N.Y.: Península Publishing Co., 1982.

To David, Peter, and Michael Glenn

Contents

xi Foreword

xv Introduction

Poems Before Easter

3 Provision

4 Traces in a river rock

5 Burning the Fields

6 Nocturne

7 Two Poems for Easter

Stories

11 Ismene

13 Meditation

14 Thinking of Hawks

15 A Story

16 Come wordless . . .

16 Faulty Sonnet

17 In the Great Wheel

17 The Princess Waking, After a Hundred Years

18 One Last Song

19 For R. G. S., Dead by His Own Hand

20 Faustus

21 Persephone

23 Crossing Water

23 You, reading me a poem long-distance

24 Sequence: Biographical

24   QUITTING

24   IN THE SHADOW

24   CARILLON: FUGUE

24   TO YOU, AWAY ON THE MOUNTAIN

24   ALONE TOGETHER

25 Sequence: A Season of War
25   NOVEMBER 1972
26   "NOW IS THE WINTER . . ."
26   FEBRUARY
27   MARCH LETTER
27   FOR THE RECORD
28   LINES FOR PARTING
29 Bracelet, POW / MIA
29 Hendrix
30 The Hero
32 The Promise: Words for a Seder
34 The door behind me open: Words for a teacher
34 Memory

Making a World

37 Waking in Darkness, Making a World
38 The Wedge
39 Retreat
40 Correspondence
41 Letter
42 Sequence: One Day
42   #1
42   #2
43   #3
44 Herbal
44 Lines with a book of Renaissance poems
45 To Speak to Someone Grieving
46 October Evening

Portraits

51 Marriage
52 Weather
53 Still Life
53 Party—II
54 Loners
54 Together
55 Like a Waterfall
55 Penelope, Afterwards

56 Anne Fairfax to her husband, the Lord General Thomas Fairfax, 1645

58 The Marschallin

59 On Reading the Old Captivity Narratives

60 Deerslayer

To Give You Words

63 To Give You Words

65 Encounter

65 Then

66 Moebius Strip

66 Lie Down

67 Touch

68 Icarian

69 Sequence: Sleepwalk and Waking

69   SLEEPWALK

70   "HORS DE CE MONDE . . ."

71   AVALANCHE

72   NIGHTMARE

73   TURNING THE CORNER

74   REMEMBRANCE

75 Aubade

76 "Yes Is This Present Sun . . ."

77 Wishing We Were . . .

78 Fall: North of Boston

78 Picnic: Palo Alto

79 Old Friend

Envoi

83 Further On

83 This book, these words

84 Accompaniment

85 Lines with a book of poems, selections marked

86 Translations

86   EN LA MUERTE DE CRISTO, CONTRA LA DUREZA DEL CORAZON DEL HOMBRE

87   ON CHRIST'S DEATH, AGAINST MAN'S HARDNESS OF HEART

88 PINTURAS DE BATIK-COLLAGES Y POEMAS
89 BATIK-COLLAGES AND POEMS
104 HAMBRE
105 HUNGER
106 ORACIÓN
107 PRAYER
108 Eurydice in Hell
109 Charlie's Girl
110 Nineteenth-Century Letters
110 MELVILLE TO HAWTHORNE, 1851
110 HAWTHORNE TO MELVILLE, 1853
111 MELVILLE, RETROSPECTIVE ON HIS WORK, 1891

Loyalties

115 Loyalties
115 The Covenanters
116 For W. B. Yeats, quoting him
117 To Sylvia Plath
119 To a Poet, A. R.
120 For Karen

Letting Go

123 Changes
123 Smoke Song
124 Night Care
124 Dune Fragments
125 "Love Is the Hardest Lesson"
125 Talking to Myself

A Memoir of Our Life Together

N. SCOTT MOMADAY

Barbara Glenn (Momaday), 1942–2008, was a woman of great presence, perception, and talent. She lived more deeply, more completely in the world than do most of us. These poems will bear that out. They are the reflections of a mind and spirit that are truly extraordinary.

I met Barbara at a summer encampment named "Anytown, USA," in the mountains above Los Angeles in 1959. She was a camper and I was a counselor. I was on my way to Palo Alto to begin my graduate work at Stanford. She was sixteen, and although I did not know until years later, the Chrysanthemum Queen of Newport Beach. She lived on Balboa Island. Before parting she asked me to give her a list of books on poetry that she should read. I casually suggested that she should consider applying to Stanford when the time came.

I was a Stegner Fellow in poetry. Barbara came to Stanford a little later—I like to think on my advice—and she too held a Stegner Fellowship. We saw each other in classes, at readings, and in the neighborhood of Stanford Village, the student housing in which we both lived. But by that time we were married to other people.

Our paths crossed many times over the years, but gradually we lost touch with each other. I returned to my homeland of the Southwest. Barbara graduated in Law from Pepperdine University and became a partner in a prestigious law firm in Los Angeles. We were both single again.

I became a scholar at the School of American Research in Santa Fe. There, on vacation from the law firm, Barbara happened into the LewAllen art gallery on Galisteo Street and saw some of my paintings on exhibit. She was told that I was living in Santa Fe, and she called me on the telephone. We met for lunch and we spent the afternoon sipping wine and catching up with each other. That was the beginning of a long and eventful courtship. Over the next few years we met frequently and traveled around the world. In 2002 I proposed to her in Paris. We were married in Brittany, and we honeymooned in Ireland. Travel was our special delight. There were delicious sojourns in Mexico, Switzerland, Germany, Italy, Spain, Russia (including Siberia), Belize, and Alaska. When we traveled by car, Barbara did the driving. She was a navigator without peer, and she stopped at every historical marker. Her interest in the world was insatiable, and her enthusiasm was infectious. She could read a book a day, and bookstores were always glad to see her coming.

In 2006 Barbara and I went for a long weekend to a favorite retreat in Taos. There she complained of stomach pains. I took her to the nearest hospital. She was diagnosed with ovarian cancer. We telephoned a physician friend who advised us to seek treatment at the University of Oklahoma medical facility in Oklahoma City, a major center for the treatment of ovarian cancer. We drove directly there from Taos. Barbara began treatment at once, and we stayed with friends until we found a suitable apartment. For more than two years we lived in Oklahoma City, and Barbara underwent chemotherapy and radiation. She fought hard for her life with dignity, bravery, hope, and a spirit that inspired everyone around her. But the cancer had advanced too far, and she died on the 20th of September 2008. At her memorial service I said, "Ours was the best of marriages, and I believe that ours will be the best of reunions." Her ashes are scattered on Rainy Mountain, an old Kiowa camping place scared to us both.

I shall refrain from heaping praise upon *Poems Before Easter*, although I am certain that this collection is worthy of high praise indeed. Perhaps objectivity cannot be expected of me. On the other hand, I have lived in the element of language, especially of poetry, for many years, and I am confident that I know distinguished poetry when I see it. Barbara's heart is in what she wrote, and the great generosity of her heart informs both the surface and the deep center of her poems. *I will not let thee go except thou bless me.* These poems are among the great blessings of our life together.

I Would Take You There

For Barbara

If you had never seen the sea,
    I would take you there,
and I would sing of the wonder
that comes upon your face.

If you had never seen the plain,
    I would take you there,
and I would show you a thousand bluebells
quaking in the wind.

If you had never heard rolling thunder,
    I would take you into silence,
and you would hear a far
weather breaking.

If you had never known my love,
    I would take you there,
and in a sea of timelessness
we would sail the constellations.

Introduction

"Distance is Savory"

KENNETH FIELDS

When it comes, the Landscape listens—
Shadows—hold their breath—
When it goes, 'tis like the Distance
On the look of Death
>   —EMILY DICKINSON, "There's a Certain Slant of Light"

The brilliant son of a friend, when he was four years old, was talking to his mother about the size of God. She said, "God is supposed to be everywhere, so he must be very big." The little boy, Adam Spohrer, replied, "Atoms are everywhere. I think God must be very small." Barbara Glenn would have liked that story on its own merits, but also because it touches on a concern central to her poems: the mystery of proximity and distance, absence and intimacy. The idea had theological implications, as in Ben Jonson's "To Heaven": "O, being everywhere, / How can I doubt to find you ever here?" It also functions in other Renaissance poems, in what may be called poems of absence. Donne in the Valedictorians uses the idea of the absent lover to great psychological advantage.

I knew Glenn as a student, friend, and Wallace Stegner Poetry Writing Fellow, and I've known her husband, now widower, Scott Momaday, even longer. Scott first met Barbara when she was 16 years old, and they married many years later, in the last years of her life, as it turned out, marked by her cancer that went into remission, returned, and eventually killed her. Her poems deal with many themes, but running through them are concerns with absence. *Poems Before Easter*, may have an uplifting sound, but it's important to remember that the period before Easter is a time of suffering and loss leading up to rebirth.

The range of her treatment of proximity and distance may be seen in these lines: "You are real, / As only the far away can truly be" ("Thinking of Hawks"). And Penelope's startling understanding of her weaving after the return of Odysseus: "A frail web, a vow–/ And yet it bides my waking here to find/ My love of a stranger, sleeping by my side." In these lines presence is absence.

Consider the plaintiveness of this sonnet, "Nocturne":

Languorous summer, when the long summer day
Fades late and almost imperceptibility
To darkness: our two voices, intertwined
In late long talk, are lost almost, not quite,

In the voices of crickets and frogs, the stream, the wind
In the trees, a rumor of angels; and silently
Our thoughts of the ways our lives might take flare upward
As briefly as the fireflies' light, as bright

As bound to earth as they, our course and pattern
Evanescent, beyond what we can see.
The hot night wind seems then the breath of God,
Too heavy to bear, impossible to flee,

Even as time, which carries us away
To separate lives from our long summer day

Another beautiful love sonnet plays inventively on her theme. I'm especially drawn to the word *contraption* for the answering machine, turned as an instrument of love:

"You, Reading Me a Poem Long-distance"

The wires sing; and this marvelous
Contraption that I have begun to love
Because it brings your voice to me,
Blinks and clicks, and turns itself on.

What magic: You gather and give to me
A wonder, a love affair with life
In forty lines or so; and you,
The resonance of all the years

I've loved you, the fierceness of my desire
To guard your distant sleeping, to be
And be yours, catch me by surprise,
Stay with me, long after the message ends

I am connected to you in ways
I have scarcely begun to understand.

These poems testify to her desire and its fulfillment in the last years of her life. After her death, Scott Momaday wrote perhaps his best poem. It appropriately enters the psychology of his late wife. "Beyond the burden of being" heartbreakingly captures the pain, now fading away, of her time before Easter.

The Snow Mare

In my dream, a blue mare loping,
Pewter on a porcelain field, away.
There are bursts of a soft commotion
Where her hooves drive in the drifts,
And as dusk ebbs on the plane of night,
She shears the web of winter,
And on the far, blind side
She is no more. I behold nothing,
Wherein the mare dissolves in memory.
Beyond the burden of being.

For Momaday, for those of us who loved Barbara, distance is distance, loss: "She is no more. I behold nothing." What we do have are these intense poems of yearning.

Poems Before Easter

Provision

i

Householders capture it in jars,
In buckets standing on the stairs
Against the failure of supply;
Or throw a dam across a stream,
Throwing the earthen trap too high,
Without success.

Even to guard against the flood
Too well, constraining a great river,
Forgoes the gift. Standing, stagnate,
Trapped, we lose the treasure:
Sweet water, or love, or God
Poured out for us.

ii

O taste and see

the rain
when the clouds burst
and the heavens open
over the thirsty earth;

the streaming fields
when the sun returns,
steam rising
into the air like prayer.

before Easter, 1987

Traces in a river rock

God only knows
the light, the wind, the rain
into which this fern
unfurled, flowered, fell back
into what secret place,
so long beneath the earth—
you hold all this
in the hollow of your hand.

So we are called
from darkness into light
and thence to darkness,
thence to the light again—
all held forever
in the hollow of His hand.

Traces in a river rock
(a type of the mind of God)
for J.T., April 14, 1987

BARBARA GLENN

Burning the Fields

Emporia, Kansas, April 1987

The fields are burning.

The smoke rises
above the ever-shifting
boundaries of siege,
low lines of flame
advancing, a brief flare
where a few tall stalks
escaped the scythes

till now. Beneath the silence
of the sky, above the silence
where the flame has passed,
the light that called us here
hangs in the smoky night,
rises to fade to darkness
beyond our sight.

So much of what we are
is grass for the fire.

Yet burning, something sweet
perfumes the still night air,
crumbles into the earth—
when the new grass leaps
into the spring,
you may taste that sweetness
on your tongue.

Nocturne

Languorous summer, when the long summer day
Fades late and almost imperceptibly
To darkness: our two voices, intertwined
In late long talk, are lost almost, not quite,

In the voices of crickets and frogs, the stream, the wind
In the trees, a rumor of angels; and silently
Our thoughts of the ways our lives might take flare upward
As briefly as the fireflies' lights, as bright,

As bound to earth as they, our course and pattern
Evanescent, beyond what we can see.
The hot night wind seems then the breath of God,
Too heavy to bear, impossible to flee,

Even as time, which carries us away
To separate lives from our long summer day.

Two Poems for Easter

I.

If this life is crucifixion, loss
After loss, hearts broken, hopes destroyed,
That is not all. That there is more
Is what we celebrate at Easter:

The Christ candle in the darkness,
The shadows long, the dark forbidding
But not finally. We see
The light the dark could not put out

Come into the world to stay, for us
The promise. And when the sunrise breaks
In light too bright to look upon,
We glimpse what these blind eyes will see

Come morning: beyond light, Light, and life
New found, restored, heart-whole, and free.

II.

for the Tuesday group

And there is more we carry with us
From Easter morning. In that light
That broke the hold of hopelessness,
Reflecting resurrection glory,

We see a world redeemed: wild flowers
Scattered across the hills like grace,
The wild green grasses, the fresh-turned fields,
A promise of summer gold and wheat.

The fragrant, broken earth is sweet
And so is human company:
The company of saints, each face
Familiar, new, so dear to us,

Bearing, imperishable, a story,
Carrying the burden of a song.

Malibu-Bodega-Malibu
Easter 1989

Stories

All sorrows can be borne if you put them into a story . . .

—ISAK DINESEN

Ismene

All of the stories that you hear are mine.
When we were young, my sister and my brothers,
I was the mother, weaving stories to keep
The dark at bay, our parents' doom, our own,
To fill their absences, the silences
That fell when we were taken unaware.

Exiled, on dusty roads I posed my stare
Against the stares of strangers, bartered for shelter
With stories of wonders I had never seen.
It was my fiercest pride Antigone
Was free from care, and never guessed the price
I paid for bread and wine. I kept her free,

My proud young sister whom I could not save.
When we returned, our father, brothers dead,
She knew too well I would remain, remember,
Faithful to pity, held by love and shame.
Now for my uncle's pain my stories weave
Forgetfulness; I keep my memories

Alone. They tell my stories in the town—
Antigone yet lives, a shepherd's wife
In the far hills, and Creon's son is king
Beyond the sea and will return. Ismene?
She is the daughter to the king's old age,
Keeping the future and the past at bay,

And all the dead. Listen—sometimes at night
I creep from the walls of town to the cave's stopped mouth
Unseen, and tear at the massive blocks of stone,
Her tomb, until my fingertips are torn
And weep as I will not. My sister's blood
Shines on the silent stones above my head,

Her life and mine, beyond my stories' reach.
I fall to my knees in the dark and dream of power,
A lion's body with a woman's face,
Ismene, rising on gryphon's wings,
Spewing in riddling anger an end to stories
In truth, in fire, down on the sleeping town.

But there is no end to stories in riddling truth,
Only the going on that ends in truth
Beyond our stories' end. The rising sun
Touches the far hills with darkness and with light,
Calls me to rise and go. When I am gone
The stories that you hear will be your own.

Meditation

Paolo and Francesca turn
forever separate, rising and falling
in the vortices of Dante's hell,

lovers who loved once, desire
imprisoned in nothingness
at God's pleasure, apart from God.

Now Dante's book is closed,
and rockets penetrate the spheres
of song, space has no end

or center, the hegemony of heaven
is pulled down. Yet restless
still, in the misted glass

of art and time, the guilty lovers
turn and rise and fall, inscribing
the double helix in our blood;

we turn in Cartesian vortices
of vast indifference, and love
is an unstable configuration in the void.

Thinking of Hawks

Blank walls about me shut me out,
And insubstantial flesh that will not give,

Blank faces come too close to think
They smile, or even see. But late at night

These dreams that trouble day depart:
I shut my eyes, I breathe the air we share,

I do not doubt you. You are real,
As only the far away can truly be:

The hawks, so far away they are
The angle of their wings against the sky.

A Story

for Scott

You see, the way it happened was this:
Two people, they were made for each other
Although they did not know that yet,
Not yet. These two, they came together
Years before they became themselves,
Yet what they were to be, as yet
Unknown to each of them, they apprehended
In each other. A piece of each other
They took away from that encounter,
And when they met again, years later,
They had for each other a gift: *See,*
I have for you the best of me;
I did not know I had carried you with me
Deep in my heart, these many years,
And now I can give you back yourself
As you were, and are, and are meant to be.

Come wordless . . .

For all that I have made
my life of words
there is a part of me
that would leave words,

shed wit, and wariness,
and come to you
whom I have always loved
with all my heart,

come wordless.

Faulty Sonnet

Coming together, I leave with you
A piece of myself, so that, in time,
I am not myself entirely,
Apart from you.

You, who are so complete in yourself
Alone, entire, a continent
I could explore for the rest of my life,
Is it, that you are complete only

Apart from me? That coming together
You risk the loss of what you are,
You lose (or somehow think you lose)
A piece of yourself?
                        Take me in:
If then I have a piece of you,
You have yourself; you have me too.

In the Great Wheel

Somewhere, someplace
I married you
And danced with you

In the solemn circle
Treading time

Somewhere, someplace
I carried your life in me
And bore your death

In such transactions
There is an exchange of souls:

I am your shield
And you are mine.

for Scott
February 1991

The Princess Waking, After a Hundred Years

My body is awake, and wants you. I
Just want to die. Half sleeping, half awake,
I do not know if I can break the spell
That is my story, a cinema verité
In which I am touched, I feel, I am abandoned,
All without pictures, without sound.

From the tears I cried in my long sleeping,
These briars have grown that now imprison me;
And I who never wanted to be free
Will tear myself to pieces on their thorns.

One Last Song

Don't tell me you don't love me.
Don't tell me you don't want to see
Where love might take us,
Where our lives might go
If we threw caution and common sense away
Instead of what we have together.

Tell me you do not know
Where love might take us,
Tell me you do not know
If what I see in you
Or what you see in me
Is really there.

Tell me you are afraid
Of what we might do, one to another;

Don't tell me you don't care.

For R. G. S., Dead by His Own Hand

Each dying friend that I am with
reminds me to let my heart be torn open,
that love never dies.

—STEPHEN LEVINE

When I awake tomorrow morning
You will be gone. You have been gone,
Wherever the beloved, longed-for dead
Are gone, for some time now, withdrawn

Beyond the tapestry of days
Where I look and wonder, wordlessly,
That there is no absence where you were
And therefore feel your loss anew.

Tomorrow morning when I wake
My heart will be whole before I rise,
As before all beginning we surmise
The child's heart whole, because the child

Cannot imagine the heart at all.
Am I then to let my heart
Be torn, discover anew each day
Love never dies? I would prefer

That love might die, that you might live
My friend, in the casual passages
Of every day, so we might care
For one another as we can.

Faustus

He escaped
the common lot, the thickening
of his young love's form
in childbirth, the loss
of his own flesh quickening
to danger, or to love

Because he dreamed
not only Helen, but Paris too
and Marguerite, a thousand dreams
he entered, tasted, knew, became
the catamite of his own designs,
the endless pure geometries
of pleasure, and of pain.

The price? Dreams cannot be
the stuff of memories
rising like fires in an old love's eyes,
love's body, fired in the kiln of age
yet still the sure vessel of desire.
The common lot escaped him
in the end; he knew
he had known nothing finally
to keep, to lose.

Persephone

It was the springtime. Springing from darkness, crocus
And hyacinth, violets, aster, all the flowers
Above the fresh earth turned by the forcing buds,
Dark loam against rain-beaten winter brown—
The swell of darkness opened again to birth
The spring stays in my thought when all the colors
Of flowers scarce sun-touched are long since gone.
It was the dark fresh earth, the mystery
Of spring that called me there, I think—untaught,
Untouched by dark experience, drawn there
To gather flowers as any girl unwitting,
To deck a bridal bed, garland with flowers
The mystery of love and birth. I dreamed
A young man followed me across the fields. . . .

And then the dark earth opened, and all the force
That had broken winter's hold came on me, took me,
Loosed my hair, my garments, crushed my flowers
And then I knew no more. I woke in darkness,
Knowing my love my death, the scent of flowers
Crushed as heavy as the fresh-turned earth,
And I was inconsolable. I wept.
Never to come to summer, to harvest, to know
Sweet mingled ordinary pain and joy,
Never to be an old crone dressed in black,
My springtime pressed in the shadows of memory,
Dreaming in winter sun. . . .

               It is the springtime.
I walk your fields, weeping—weeping for all
That passes so quickly in your sunlit lives,
Weeping for all that will never come to me.
You hail me, follow me out across the fields—
The soft spring rains I am, the crocus and aster,

Hyacinth, violets, all the flowers crushed
And broken by your plows. You look to harvest,
You see the summer springing—let me go.
I lost long ago what you find here each spring,
And what I find is not for you to seek.
The swell of darkness opened again to birth
My end in this beginning holds my thought;
I only long to go down to the darkness again.

Crossing Water

The stream, rain-swollen:
the sounds of water
drown the memory
of crackling leaves, dry
grass beneath my step
just yesterday.
        This
is to realize
the power of water
to divide: I crossed
with such temerity before.

You, reading me a poem long-distance

The wires sing; and this marvelous
Contraption that I have begun to love
Because it brings your voice to me,
Blinks and clicks, and turns itself on.

What magic! You gather and give to me
A wonder, a love affair with life
In forty lines or so; and you,
The resonance of all the years

I've loved you, the fierceness of my desire
To guard your distant sleeping, to be
And be yours, catch me by surprise,
Stay with me, long after the message ends.

I am connected to you in ways
I have scarcely begun to understand.

Sequence: Biographical

QUITTING

Two things I needed,
cigarettes and you—
two things I'm learning
now to do without.
This morning I woke
up, to full ashtrays
and an empty life.

IN THE SHADOW

Love is the noon:
to celebrate
as it is gone.

CARILLON: FUGUE

The day in flight!
These bells allay
the fall to night.

TO YOU, AWAY ON THE MOUNTAIN

Far, the mountain peak:
it is the valley
to the peak beyond.

ALONE TOGETHER,

one definition—
there is no other,
you are not alone.

Sequence: A Season of War

NOVEMBER 1972

Due to circumstances
beyond our control
a truce is cancelled.
Still, the management
says that peace is sure:
unprecedented
success in saving
life is in our grasp.
Machines will target,
drones destroy: the mark,
objectively, is
anything that lives.
There is no limit.
There is no risk of
lives. American
efficiency will
end the war, they say,
and I believe them:
we can end it all.
The automated
air war promises
sure peace: I fear that
we will come to crave
that nothingness, that
peace, no life at all.

"NOW IS THE WINTER . . ."

There was a time we thought to lose ourselves
In something larger than ourselves.

That was the loss of loneliness in words.
It felt like life. Yet this is life,

This tiredness and numbness of the mind
Foreshadowing rest, the longed-for end.

FEBRUARY

This is the ebb of the year:
not the rush of spring or fall
nor fullness of late summer.
The snows that broke at full flood
wave on wave against the hills,
obliterating every
landmark, have receded now.
The earth lies bare. In hollows,
the snowmelt tidal pools are
waiting for the surge, the green
spring tides again returning
to cover these inland shores.

In February, waiting
for the future is not our
personal predicament,
not we alone; it is the
shared communion of the whole.

MARCH LETTER

A cloudy day.
Buried in work,
I had not thought of you
till now
the sun and shower
break the winter's hold
together, and
your care
falls on me,
like this rain.

FOR THE RECORD

Yes
we know
the worth of love
the warmth of home
the joy in friends
and celebrations
that we share.

Still we must go.
The odds are long—
so long
we dare risk
nothing less.

LINES FOR PARTING

Shall we love each other now
before we go? Let us take
the old familiar ways,
finding what we know so well
again in the discoveries
of each other's bodies. Come
let us find the little death
together—then we may part,
without fear in the shadow
of the deaths we die alone.

Bracelet, POW/MIA

for all the prisoners

Name, rank, and serial number, stamped
impersonally on steel: being
a man you do not know. Do you know
the weight he bears? What weight to you,
this claim to share his narrow place? Such
intimacy, worn on the wrist, seems
a safe distance.
                              It the real touches
you, there is a band you wear unseen,
unsought cold metal about the heart.
Asian moonlight falls through your windows,
lies on late night wakefulness, and there
you may see the shape of what you know,
barred in shadows on the empty floor.

Hendrix

In a world where all we wanted was to get it right
Before it all came down, he was the one:

The short fuse, the resistance at the amp,
Taking the experience that we were deadened to,

Fusing the meaning and the sound of who we were—
The bombs, the rockets, in the harsh lights' glare

Even the dream of freedom we were afraid to share.
He got it right, before it all came down.

The Hero

i. *directions*
   To make up the meaning
   of ourselves: a discipline of
   sternness and simplicity
   and an absolutely untheatrical
   feeling for life—
   this last, not quite.
   A feeling for the theatre
   of here, of what we do,
   is a controlled release
   from knowing
   there is no certainty.
   We know
   this is a limited engagement.

   Security
   of a sort is found
   at sea, or in the air—
   in the secure unknown.
   Its dangers and its disciplines
   we learn, leaving the land;
   its terrors demand no more
   than our resistance
   and final resignation.

ii. *caveat*

At one or two
when energy burns low
and breathing slows, and hesitates,
and one is almost conscious of
the choice before each indrawn breath,
we know we do not know
what time is left.

We tell our numbers silently,
as the devout tell beads.
A circle of ourselves
is a safe place—
the dark we fear
is where we go alone.

iii. *epitaph for someone else*

He was alive, which meant
he hurt. He loved
other people, without regard to
who they were
or what they knew—
he only knew their need.
There is nothing more
to say, except that he
insisted on reality,
and that was right, of course,
but hardly viable.

The Promise
Words for a Seder

i

      Why is this night unlike
All other nights? We eat in haste,
Move restlessly from room to room,
Touching the pieces of our years
Here, books, a print, a photograph
Long-kept but never truly seen
Till now. There are no more words to say.
There is a journey in the air.

We wait. But there will be no knock,
No word, and this is not the night:
Yet this night, every night to come
Until we go, is resonant
With what will be when this is past,
The long remembrance of the night
When we have gone at last.

ii

The herbs are bitter—desert herbs
And salt, the taste
Of separate journeys to this place,
Of lonely journeys yet to make.

In this time, stolen from time, still
The taste of our captivity
Is on our lips,
Although we will not speak of it.

iii
The careful warmth, the quiet place, the time
For bread to rise, for what we share to grow
Into the daily substance of our lives,
All this we leave behind. The bread we have
Is yet our stay, our sustenance and staff.

iv
Rejoice! Tonight, recline—
In music, food, and wine,
The presence of these friends.
Take ease, for there is more
Than journeying to come.

Rejoice tonight! Recall
And celebrate in all
We share, the promised end—
A promise here, before
Our coming home.

The door behind me open
Words for a teacher

for Roy Bundy

I hope when I am older
I will not impose myself
upon near strangers' wisdom,
dearly won.
                But since I took
from you, I wanted to say
this for you to hear:
                        I see.
And I am out of the room
that I had locked myself, and
I have left the door behind
me open.
                I want to see
behind me open doors, and
I want to leave (though no one
sees) the last door open too.

Memory

Though now the torch of days
Assays our sorrow's coin,
Burning away the dross,
This metal of the past
Will long extend, a wire
Gold-bright and threaded through
Our loss.
                It is our own,
Gain of the present fire,
Ours for the ferryman,
Our payment, Charon's due.

Making a World

Waking in Darkness, Making a World

Waking in darkness from deep sleep
And dreaming, the disembodied watcher
Wakes from his visions to the real,
Feels the closed eyelids of the night
Upon his open eyes, a blindness
Between sleep and waking thought.

These words were thought then, in the darkness,
Wakeful before the dawn, and the thinker
Was Thought, perhaps, waking in darkness
To make up the dawn to come.

The Wedge

Newport Beach, California

I think of going back again, of finding
The way I made my own once, long ago,
Out of my landlocked self to absolutes
Of surge and undertow and surge again.

I think of standing, back to the jetty rocks,
Where the sounding swell and crash of surf gives way
To the soft susurrus of its ebbing flow,
Ever the sea drawn back to the sea again.

There where I sought the sea once, long ago,
I think of going back, as if it were
A salt elixir I might taste, and know
Myself there in the place from which I came,

But that was long ago. I think of rising
Seas in late August, late in the afternoon,
The swelling storm surf towering out of the sun,
Touched with fire, higher than my head.
Even the jetty is no refuge then—
It sounds, a muffled anvil in the flood.

And I have tasted the salt of my own blood,
Have been borne down in the darker surge and tow
Of inward seas. I know myself, afraid—
I think of going back, but will not go.

Retreat

In the deep coolness of this place,
The fossil-fern forgot by time
Is rooted at the redwoods' base,
Persistent, by no thought confined.

The redwoods tower out of mind.
Reflecting nothing in the shade,
There is a small clear pool to bind
All changeless here. Yet thought may fade:

I came here out of a sunny clime,
Out of a spring too soon returned,
Seeking a place where I might find
Lost winter memories. I learned,

Even in timeless shade and space,
The mind is bound to change and time,
And time will solace, time erase
The mind's forgetting, and the mind.

Correspondence

i

It is some time now we have lived
Apart, survivors of catastrophe
Still mercilessly blank:

Increasingly unused to speech,
Our letters are the last words to a world
Fading from memory

And hope, the messages in bottles,
Revelations of the self one casts
Into the sea.

ii

We have been out of touch. For these past months
The world has ended at my fingertips,
Holding the letters that I never sent.
What now can bridge the chasm of return?
I see you, and, before we touch, I hear
The chaos of a year's unsaid concern—
All that we will not say speaks in my ear.

Letter

Write me, that I may see your face.
I do not always understand—
I always see. You,
Sitting across from me,
Quizzical, loving, laughing a little
At what I do not understand.

Sequence: One Day

Ten thousand years is long
and so a morning and an evening count.
— MAO TSE-TUNG

#1
Remember
we were most alive
not in the brief blaze
of becoming one
but in the grace
of conscious tension,
making space between us
before separation,
making memories to keep us
most alive.

Remember that,
and we may take
another way through fire
to be most alive
and one.

#2
Soon now,
you will be here.
And I will see you,
we will reach
to hold each other,
say, "You see,
we never had to worry,"
(you are here)

and smile.
What are there,
twenty, thirty, forty years ahead?
Life is so short,
and we have all the time there is.

#3
It is not so hard this time
to return, to go once more
among accustomed places,
faces seen every day
before you came
and went away again.

There are no pieces to pick up
of the everyday
for we broke nothing here
and nothing here had changed.
Only—a day together.
Returning, everything is strange.

Herbal

Mint climbs my windowsill, to trellis
The windowbox in soft profusion,
And near a thicket of flowering chives,
Crisp parsley springs, sweet after rain.
Safe behind glass, basil and thyme
Hang drying in the winter sun.
All these are here obedient,
The outward signs of my content.

But free of my design, unruly,
The rosemary, sharp-needled and blue
As spruce on distant mountaintops,
Dusty and pungent as desert sage,
Grows into winter by my walk,
Remembrance, insurgent memory.

Lines with a book of Renaissance poems

Who is happy in this life?
The very best, beset by strife,
Have testified to loss, to grief,
To failed endeavors, failed belief,
To sins of selfishness and pride,
To friendship spurned, and love denied.
But in this world, the seasons turn.
Year after year, they bring their stern
And lovely gifts: sweet flowers remain;
Wise memory outlasts its pain.
From the best their lesson learned at last:
Time's consolations, all held fast
Within the cadences of rhyme;
Time's understanding, gained in time.

To Speak to Someone Grieving

It's true what they say, that grief
goes, even the memory
you think to keep. The rainbow
bars the sky: illusory,
it has no place, suspended
in the multiplicity
of the falling, passing rain.
But look—here are the colors
of the sun you cannot see
save in the broken light. And
listen—colors span the sky
always: you live in twilight,
even when you cannot see.

October Evening

Newport Beach, California

i
In the pale gray light
night falls even

imperceptibly
across the bay

where gray water rocks
the shrouded boats

a single gull wheels
suddenly, is

lost in mist and now
the jetty light appears

and disappears

ii
And the pearl on pearl
inlaid in mussel

shells, tall sails ghosting
home into harbor

gray on silver gray
holding the last light

silently across
the bay, the only sounds

soft slap of water
luffing sails, floating

calls, good night, good night.

Portraits

Marriage

I remember the crook of your wrist
as you bent above your notes, I watched
you, and I leaned to interrupt the
pulse-point just below your ear, to kiss
your hair, your mouth, to keep you from work
one time, again, a hundred times then
all the flavors marry on my tongue—
salty and faintly sweet, smoky, a
memory now indefinable
almost—and I speak you and you come.

Weather

Anger so palpable it fills the house
In every room to which I flee, afraid
To face your face, estranged—this is the storm
In which we both are caught. And I recall

The pilot house, Grand Isle, where we rode out
The hurricane a dozen years ago.
We had gone further than we meant that day.
There at the outpost of the rivermen,

The world was lost it seemed, the wires down
In the rising wind, and chaos come in air
And water whirled against the cypress planking,
Shuddering above the rising tides.

Dead center in the storm, a sudden space
For fear, lost in the silence and the dark,
I still remember finding you by touch
Beside me. You had been there all along,

And now the worst was over. The storm passed.
We were alive, stunned in the shining day,
The common miracle of aftermath,
As we emerged to make our way back home.

Still Life

Their legs entangled still,
The bedclothes bunched below their feet,
The lovers after love. They lie
Unseparate, neither two nor one,
Both looking to the past:
"Was this it, finally, the last
Act of despair?" The question
Weighs on their bodies, freights still air.

Party—II

The masks have slipped from faces all around me,
Or is it, all around me masks are donned
To hide the emptiness of after five?
Faces I thought familiar, voices awry
In empty lives, are filling sudden spaces
With patterns, games I do not want to join
Nor want to understand.
                                          Stranger like me,
We meet, and speak, and I have listened to you,
Saying all that is never said, and I have watched
The party all around and you unchanged.
But this is not what I would have it be
As our eyes meet—some last forlorn defense
Against this lovelessness that finds us saying,
Lonely and strangers, we are not like these.

Loners

They move in and out
of strobelight
or candlelight

looking for someone
to make a couple
to forget in the darkness

the one sitting alone
who is looking too
for someone to love

something to take down
to the darkness
whenever it comes

Together

There is no other here. At last
Found in the glass is no reflection—
Wine is an end here, at the end
Of evening, to long separation,
Losses insoluble before
And after. There will be tomorrow,
Ghosts crowding in with morning light—
No one is here to lose, tonight.

Like a Waterfall

No one doubts the power of water
Falling, filling the sky with sound,
Shaking the ground on which we stand.
We wonder at the enduring rock,
The fragile flowers blossoming
So close to the edge of nothingness;
We wonder that we stand so close
To the force of the cataract and live.

We know in our bones it cannot cease,
But should we come one day to silence,
As it to a death that should not be,
Who has the will to climb the cliffs,
To trace the dry and stony course,
To search for the hidden springs that failed?

Penelope, Afterwards

Often at night I pick the pattern out,
In dreams undoing the warp and woof of all
The days gone by. Weaving, unweaving, no doubt
Of my lord assailed me then—I dreamed him, tall
And strong, as I remembered him at leaving;
Like the bed he made of the living olive tree
He stayed with me through all the years of grieving,
In dreams deep-rooted as my loyalty,

Or so I thought. I wake from dreaming now
To wonder at my weaving, the tangled ties
Of loyalty, remembered love and time,
The pattern set. A frail web, a vow—
And yet it bides my waking here to find
My love a stranger, sleeping by my side.

Anne Fairfax to her husband,
the Lord General Thomas Fairfax, 1645

The air is heavy in the garden,
Heavy the deep red roses hold
The garden close, and in deep summer
The apple trees beyond the wall
Dream in the timeless heat and hum
Of the turning year. Nun Appleton
Enfolds me, Thomas, without solace.
Heavy is time for me, and heavy
My thoughts of you, my husband, away
Where the war wastes into another year,
Wasting the flowers and fields of England
While far to the north, foreboding, storms
Of a colder season of war to come
Cloud time's horizon. You have my heart
As surely as when my father gave me
Into your care, as when you brought me
Here to this garden where I learned
To love you, your rare laughter, love
And our daughters in the sun. But war
And harder lessons have come between
That time and now. Your letter tells
Of Will your brother, dead, whom I
Loved next to you, and I come today
From the cottages of our own folk
To which the men will not return.
Gazing at garden peace unseeing,
I see the Bradford weavers still,
Who followed you when you went south.
How many Bradford men will see
Their looms again? When the baby died,
It seemed I left you, but your need,
And little Moll's, recalled me home.
But Will, and the others, all our own—

No matter our resolve, our faith,
The cause we share—we are apart.
A country's length lies hard between
Your need and mine. Must we belong
More to these dead than to each other?
More than your faith and honour, more
Than Cromwell and the right keep you
And your standard in the south; more
Than my loneliness and love for you
Weigh on me here. The roses are
Blood red, the last of the apple blossoms
Are withered where they fell. I long
For your return, but I pray God
For mercy, more than He has shown
To England yet, that I may learn
Again to love, that we again
May find each other beyond lost laughter,
In peace in a garden, in the sun.

The Marschallin

You say to me that life is ours to keep,
That we are meant to hold all that we love
Encompassed in our hearts. I too was young—
I can remember thinking so. It seems
As near now as this day falling to night,
It seems just yesterday I held, heart-whole,
Within myself the world. But now to you
I say life is a matter of heart-breaking,
Fragment by fragment giving to love all love
Can bear, and in the inescapable
Particular—a time, a place, a man.
Time passes. Times and places, and the men,
Pass as they must. I knew myself in giving—
I know myself alone by what is gone.
I know there may be more—that, we shall see.

On Reading the Old Captivity Narratives

for J. L. W.

In the old frontier narratives of captivity
There is always the scene—the clearing,
The ruined cabin, perhaps no more left
Than the stones of a chimney, morning mist rising
Above cold ashes, and the dead
For whom all is over. Someone is missing
And someone is grieving, left behind.
Is this where my child, my lover was taken?

It is the beginning of the tale. The trail
Is as cold as the ashes, the search as long
As love and memory and hope, a chimera cold
As morning mist. The tales follow the captives,
And the searchers' quests are nearly always doomed.
Love passes, memory fails in long captivity
The stories say, but life goes on—there joy is found,
Even if it is not what one would choose.

Only the searchers were prisoners forever
In the old frontier narratives of captivity.
Those were wisest, left behind, who relinquished
Their hope and grieving, buried their missing with their dead,
Recorded their memories and built their lives and loves anew.
Hard wisdom there is in these old pages, hard-won
On dark and bloody ground—there is joy to be found
In living, even if it is not what we would choose.

Deerslayer

What matter if when I was young,
Mine was the deathsong that my bullets sung?
For I shot true. My gift was good:
I was my final quarry as I stood.

To Give You Words

To Give You Words

i

What of these words we say?
Words tumbling of themselves,
Spilled in the space between
Two friends, can make a wall
Between two strangers. We
Are friends. We risk ourselves,
Endanger what we mean
Each to the other, all
We are each time we speak.

ii

A gesture is a sort
Of word. Though not precise,
Lacking the edge of speech,
Though it cannot define,
It cannot hurt. It is
A bridge between.

                      The brush
Of a hand, a look returned,
Fragile and tenuous,
Ephemeral, these still
Surprise us, make us one
In promise, unfulfilled
Yet ever rebegun.

iii

More difficult than love,
This being friends. You come
And go away again,
Your way your own, that I
Can never know. Love knows
No time, no loneliness;
One lives in love as in
The warmth of summer days
That have no end. To be
A friend is to endure
The winter, is to trust
In summer in the spring's
Slow tentative return.

Encounter

What can I do with this?
The difficulty is
In what is not quite said,
For eyes are eloquent
With all that the dreaming head
Can hold, the heart betray.
What then? The words we will,
We will not ever say.
Love is to human scale,
Rooted in time and place;
Sudden, diffuse, desire
Is measureless, slow fire.

Then

You kissed me
and I was afraid
a little
because it meant so much.
We had come to this
in months of talk,
of times and places shared,
easy at distances,
sometimes so close
we had to look away.
All that we were
to one another
meant so much to me—
and now
always a part of me
would be waiting for your kiss.

Moebius Strip

I was desperate-
ly unhappy
late last night

and woman-like
I fixed on this

I didn't know
where to find you

by which I meant

would you ever come
looking for me?

Lie Down

Kneeling over me you put
your hand on the small of my back
so near, your breathing warm in my ear
to say lie down, my sweet, and I did

I wanted to, sink gratefully
into your voice's tenderness
your hand in touch, into release
I wanted to lie down, give up

the struggle to stand alone
hearing your voice as I hear it now
feeling alone the air's caress
saying what is, and is to come

lie down, lie down.

Touch

i

How hard you fight it
being loved

you are a man
and you demand
I let you be

but I think of
a little boy
I held, once
though he fought me

fighting
until his head
fell to my shoulder
and he slept

ii

Love
should be something to rest in

come to as a fire
after a rainy walk

the warm sand come to
from October surf

the touch of a hand
you know by heart

Icarian

The difficulty of speech
when the dark comes down
at the end of the day, and distance
means words stretched along a wire

when what I see
is many-layered
(sea, horizon, sky)
and should be spoken, heard

at once, all at one time
I fall—
fall silent—
sky, horizon, sea.

Sequence: Sleepwalk and Waking

SLEEPWALK

The phone rings, and you ask me
why I am crying
and I cannot pretend:
my life is there, not here—

not in the dream time
not in the nightmare time
when dreams are gone and reality
stalks the prey we have become by dreaming—

my life is there. A phone call
and I am there. I will be there
and you will not, only
you will be, just beyond—

the phone call that never comes
the dream just at the edge
of nightmare where I walk alone
the last thought grasped, escaping, waking—

I wake every time
the phone rings, every time.

"HORS DE CE MONDE . . ."

A thousand miles away
trapped here
as I hang up the phone

I want to be
where you can see me
catch me up, take me along—

an old song, fainter now
long distance. The past
is static, the connection's bad—

an old sad song
(catch me up, take me along)
you cannot see me.

I was not sad once
and I want to be
anywhere but here.

AVALANCHE

it's like being dead
only I'm alive somewhere
trapped inside
to know it . . .

is it ever like this
for you too?
was it ever like this
for you?

terrible
this human wish
to share

pain
or nothingness
rather than nothing at all

NIGHTMARE

Let it roll over you—you wake
and remember and wish you slept
again, all those years

of dreaming and only nightmares
now return. Let it roll over you—
disgust and pain, more hurt

than just your pride, you needed
much too much to wake
so soon. Too late for pride

you wake—let it turn and tumble
all you dreamed you were—
it will pass

and you will still be here.

TURNING THE CORNER

Waking up these mornings, gray
on the sunniest days, afraid to move
like someone a long time sick—

waiting for pain to settle in
with waking, hoping it won't
this morning, that some small

vagrant joy will light a moment,
a promise on a pillowslip,
not slip away—

you're still pretty sick
my mama said, when you lie
awake unmoving,

trying to guess what recovery
might be like, what lies ahead
is still a long way off.

REMEMBRANCE

Afterwards
trying to re-
member, put back
together, see
in my mind's eye the whole

And, before me
the shattered
scattered pieces,
this empty egg-
shell fractured

Never to hold you again?
No.
Better,
never forget.

Aubade

To wake to see
you looking at me
sidelong, and sleepy-eyed
as always, wide awake,
one arm behind your head—

To wake to fit
myself, eyes closed,
close to your sleeping back
against the steady sleeping
rhythm of your breathing—

Perhaps these were
the most precious times,
alone with the beloved sleeping,
each guarding each other's breathing
in our own so different ways—

God knows. I know
I wake, eyes closed,
to know that you lie waking
somewhere as the day is breaking,
and I wonder what you see.

September 1982

"Yes Is This Present Sun . . ."

It can never be satisfied, the mind, never.
                                    —Wallace Stevens

Just as I feel your sidelong glance
Warm on my skin, cool at my back
The shadow is where I'm alone.

Toward warmth from darkness is instinctive
Motion, the music of the spheres:

Already as I turn to you
I'm afraid of falling, afraid of the dark
Vast silences between the stars

When you and your warm glance are gone.

July 1982

Wishing We Were . . .

Casablanca, 1942

I was wishing we were
film, as I watched you go
receding down the road
the months, the years
out of my life, but not
kindly.
                 Wishing we were film
because then you and I were
incandescent—see
love find itself, the last
and first of nights, the end
and the beginning—see
in film that moment
still there, near as the years
that will pass, have passed, near
as the end that finally
cannot impose itself between.

May 1982

Fall: North of Boston

For Bruce and Janet

Rockport Sunday, was it really so long ago?
A drive up the coast, you two had located every
Literary landmark, and I couldn't understand what kept
Those writers at their desks, houses tight shut
Against the dazzling light, the glint of gray sea,
Backs turned to the pungent material tangle of nets
And sheds and sky, bright colors fresh-weathered, the wash
On the line, the work of Salem's more practical souls.

And now you have two children I've never seen:
I remember the crisp dry air, the wind off the water,
The cafe, its white walls plastered with tattered notices
The only signs of crowds now two months gone,
Frosty breath, red cheeks and noses, frozen fingers—
          I've never been so warm.

Fall 1978

Picnic: Palo Alto

Say that we loved each other,
Lay together, watched
The clouds chase shadows across
The velvet hills as winter
Turned to spring, returned
To each other as often as
We turned away, shared everything
We knew. Nothing is permanent—
No one could ask for more.

Fall 1979

Old Friend

I wanted to make you a poem
full of honesty and all the raw edges
of what we are, but the forms of words
come too easily to me, and the discipline
of living comes too hard. I cannot
really look at what is real
and do anything else: not in these words
do we come together. Below this making
is wordless memory, the darkness of entering
the self and the other, the slow return.

Old friend, old friend
we hurt each other, we invade
each other, we use each other,
we are each other's scars
and strength. We know each other
and we are still here.
Apart, together
our roots reach down into darkness,
we reach for light.

Envoi

Further On

Abandoning each day
to risk the next

in darkness
huddled over the coals in rain
to hear them hiss and die

stirring the ashes cold
and setting out
before the cold stars wane

each day depends
on finding further on

a stranger with the gift of fire

This book, these words

pebbles dropping
into a still clear pool
make circles widening
and circles crossing circles
till the surface holds a web of light
reflecting light
on faces which lean to look
themselves held in the wonder
of a web of light
your face and mine
and all the faces of our loves

all of us dropping pebbles
in circles widening
the web these words
perhaps this book

Accompaniment

i
How strange it is
to go without you

finding everything you taught me once
to look for

strange
to find you here

the descant on discovered joy

ii
Again
        again the strands
descant and obligato

turn and counterturn
wind through the fugue

poised at the rest
how did I think
I would go on alone

Lines with a book of poems, selections marked

for aam

In this happen-
stance and circumstance
of poems you will find
the instance—these poems bound and free
(even as we) are yours
my Russian friend are you

even as in deep winter
above the Nevsky Prospect Chagall soars
over the huge dome of Saint Isaac the high spires
of the admiralty Russian
as frostbound melancholy
riding the giddy light
air rising above the weight of cold
and the horseman in the square

poems bursting overhead bouquets of flowers
tugging at their moorings to the ground—
smile friend at folly
of unhappiness and happiness alike.
Alone with these? no not
(not ever) alone.

Translations

EN LA MUERTE DE CRISTO,
CONTRA LA DUREZA DEL CORAZON DEL HOMBRE

—FRANCISCO DE QUEVEDO

Pues hoy derrama noche el sentimiento
por todo el cerco de la lumbre pura,
y amorticido el sol en sombra obscura
da lagrimas al fuego y voz al viento;

pues de la muerte el negro encerramiento
descubre con temblor la sepultura,
y el monte, que embaraza la llanura
del mar cercano, se divide atento:

de piedra es, hombre duro, de diamante
tu corazon, pues muerte tan severa
no anega con tus ojos tu semblante.

Mas no es de piedra, no; que si lo fuera,
de lastima de ver a Dios amante,
entre las otras piedras se pompiera.

ON CHRIST'S DEATH,
AGAINST MAN'S HARDNESS OF HEART

—FRANCISCO DE QUEVEDO

Because this day spills forth on all the world
The final night, framed in eternal ire,
The sun dark-shadowed, deadened, voices hurled
Against the wind in vain, tears lost in fire;

And now that the black dungeon deeps of death
Gape wide to show their terror, and the tomb,
And at the sight the brazen mount is cleft
And falls, no more above the sea to loom:

You are of stone, proud man, of diamond
Your heart, that death so terrible can prod
No tears to flood your face in some like token.

You are not even stone; he who will lend
His grief when he beholds the love of God
Will with the stones be called, with them be broken.

—MYRIAM DIOCARETZ

"La Mujer de Hoy"

"Sal de entre las piedras y muros, el caos, la obscuridad, la confusíon en que has permanecido hasta ahora a causa de tradiciones y mitos que te son ajenos. Estás caída, acallada, casi ciega. Ten la valentía de enfrentar al mundo a pesar de estar fragmentada puesto que, desnuda y sin otra arma que tu propio yo, eres aún poderosa. En otros lugares las mujeres han despertado hacia la dignificación de su condición humana, cultural y social.

De ti depende encontrar tu propio camino."

1. *"tejedora de la paz"*

alguien la llamo
     "tejedora de la paz"
pero ella siente sue filos
     dispuestos a atacar
en cualquier ciudad

    la mujer
    es el ser
    con una misión
      definida

la mujer es el contacto
    el lugar
      de la vida

—MYRIAM DIOCARETZ

From Woman Today

"Emerge from your narrow cells, from the chaos, obscurity, and shame in which you have been imprisoned until now by myths and traditions not your own. You are oppressed, silenced, nearly blind. But you have the courage to confront the world, shattered as you are—empty-handed, weaponless, you are still strong. In other places, women have awakened to claim that dignity of the human condition in culture and society which is rightfully theirs.

It is up to you to find the way which is your own."

1. *The weaver of peace*

someone called her
    the weaver of peace
but she knows the knives
    poised to attack her
in any city you might name

    a woman
    is born
        to a singular
    vocation

        the lightning-rod
    and ground
        of life

2. Sombras silentes

¿Quien
    llegará
    al pretil
del invisible puente
    donde
    cada
    mujer
espera que transcurran
    las grises
    y
    silentes
    sombras,
a estrenar
    el acto
    germinal
de las inéditas horas?

3. ¿Dónde te encuentras?

¿Hacia
    dónde
    vas,
extraviándote
por las avenidas
de ingenua
    irrealidad,
confundida
    por el placer
de tan solo circular?

2. In the shadows

Who
    will stand watch
    at the battlements
of the invisible bridge
    where
    every woman's
    hopes
are passing
    grey
    and
    silent
    shades?

Who will begin
    the first
    song
of the unsung hours?

3. Where do you find yourself?

Where
    are
    you going,
losing yourself
in the byways
of your foolish
    fantasy,
bedazzled
    by the pleasure
of your endless promenade?

4. Creación

Desciendo descalza a los campos
de quietos follajes
                    por el camino
serpenteado
el aire
        de aromos se perfuma
        en un remolino
de privada violencia

—se oye la diana—

el valle
        de lienzo
                    explota en burbajas
empapando a los cielos con púrpuras
furias
en el horizonte
        nace una forma humana
        y
        crece
        mas allá de
        la razón.

4. Creation

Descending barefoot to the plains
of quiet abundance
              by the winding
road
in the air
     the scent of myrrh
     a whirlwind
of secret violence

—time is called—

the valley
     on the canvas
          explodes a deluge
storming the heavens in purple
fury
at the horizon
     appears a human form
     born
     beyond
     all reason.

5. *Yo*

En un tumulto
de crueles dudas
me agrieto—
pero burlando al miedo
fragmento
tras
fragmento
me
    in
    ter
    no
        en el mundo
Esta
simple rime rutinaria
pronto será llama.

Mis inquietos deseos
des
    cien
        den
como lava fresca
abrumando
    tinieblas
derribando
    muros
hasta inundar todo
    con mi rayo sumo
que veo
    al
    fin

5. Self

In a tumult
of cruel doubts
I am caught—
but eluding fear
fragment
by fragment
I find
    in my
    inmost
    self
        all the world
    my
    name
common habitual rhyme
that will be flame.

My restless desire
downwards

bursts
    into
        flame
like molten lava
overwhelming
    the night
overrunning
    the height
all illuminating
    with my primal lightning
    I see
    at
    last

6. Tribulación

Soy una mujer sin nombre,
    sin cielo,
cantando por las calles
             de los hombres,
     sin
     pueblo,
observando los rostro
          esparcidos—

     Voy
         siguiendo
     mi
   propio
camino

6. Burden

I am a woman without a name,
    without sky,
singing through the streets
              of men
        without
        a people of my own,
watching the masquers
              and the merrymakers—

        I am
            going
      my
   own
way

7. Oasis

Por confundir latitudes
    peregrina
    de mi larga angustia
    fui

salvando
    de palabra
        en palabra
a las ilusiones
de la fragua
avancé hacia la arena húmeda
de huellas fatigada
cobijando ausencias
        nidos del tiempo
        en los árboles del silencio
y llegué al fin de la ruta de agua
    pare hundirme
en los fulgentes
    hontanares
    de mi única
        verdad

7. Oasis

Through the bewildering latitudes
    of boundless anguish
    I was
    a pilgrim

saving myself
    word
        by word
from fiery
illusion
I pushed my steps weary
to wet sands' coolness
sheltering absence
        eyries of time
        in the trees of silence
and came up the watercourse
    to rest at last
in the shimmering
    fountainhead
    of my singular
        truth

8. Mujer

Luego de permanecer
durante siglos
en estos pedernales
surcando
    diversos rumbos
        dando
      vueltas
        y
   vueltas
             vueltas y
          vueltas
extraviada en lo demasiado conocido
    dando tumbos—
corres por tu obscuridad y
    con el impulso de tu propia
        caída

              te encumbras

8. *Woman*

Enduring the centuries
in this hard land
your furrows are deep

         everywhere
                to and fro
       you walk
    to and fro

lost, you have seen
            too much of what you know,

    tumbling down—
you slip away into obscurity
and driven by force of your own
              fall

                 you rise

9. *"Sean la tierra y el océano . . ."*

Separe
este dolor
 el vértigo
 bajo mis pies
          en
tierra y océano

 Sea
el horizonte
lo que mis ojos recorran
en el Allá
donde todo parece acabar

 Sea
mi grito
        el viento
norte   sur
        este   oeste

 Sea
el abertal
        el lecho de
        lo nuevo
amplio
como galaxia
en el cosmos
de la mente.

9. *Genesis*
 "Let there be earth and sea . . ."

    Bury
this sadness
    below my feet
        in
earth and sea—

    I will be
the horizon
my eyes survey
yonder
where all things are possible

    I will be
the wind
    my cry
        an arrow
        to where
        all the winds
            end

    I will be
the soil
    first broken
    the seedbed of
    something new
bursting
like a galaxy
in the cosmos
of the mind.

HAMBRE

Hambre
llegas a mi puerta
encogida, tiritando,
lívida

    nos hemos vista antes
    en otra vida

y no necesito preguntar
el motivo de tu visita.

El ayuno do años
te hizo rechazar los alimentos
de otros,
porque es distinto el plato que ves
en tu delirio:

palabras frescas
humeantes
como pan caliente
en un día de mucha nieve
diciendo—
    deja todo y ven a mi lado

recibiendo su amor
en tu boca agrietada
su amor
que corre
en la tibia y luminosa
vertiente
    de su leche de mujer

HUNGER

Hunger
you approach my door
timid, trembling
pale

> we have met before
> in another life

and I do not need to ask
why you have come.

Years starving
you rejected the offerings
of others,
because it is another sustenance you seek
in your delirium:

new words
steaming
like hot bread
on a snowy day
saying
> let everything go, and come

take love
in your parched mouth
love
that streams
in the warm and shining
spring
> of the milk of woman

Juntemos las palmas.
Inclinemos nuestras cabezas.
Bajemos los párpados.

Seamos fuertes porque tratarán de separarnos.

Quédate junto a mí
mientras las aves-dudas
planean
amortajadas
ciegamente
en lo alto.

PRAYER

We join our hands.
We bow our heads.
We close our eyes.

We must be strong because they will try to part us.

Stay joined to me
While the gulls
glide
shrouded
blindly
in the sky.

Eurydice in Hell

I was not dreaming of you here, my lord,
Before you came, nor did I wake and grieve
For memories of the laughing chase, and love
Fair-caught in sunlit glades, and song. In hell,
My once-beloved, there are no marriages,
Nor love, nor hate, nor memory of pain.
The past is past and darkness covers all.
Now you come, flinging your music's blazing light
Against all the shades to claim me as your own,
I hear your song, and I know suddenly
I am in hell. The passion of the king
I feared and fled, the serpents deadly sting,
All that I had escaped possesses me
Again, and wears your form—the face of love,
Your face I once loved as my own, my life,
I cannot see. Leading me from my peace,
You are the shape of jealous passion's power,
A shade against the light that blinds my sight:
Dark Orpheus, look back, and look on me;
My lord, for what we had once, set me free.

Charlie's Girl

My father
touched me
spread my legs
rooted like a pig

My mother
held me
shushed my tears
and held me

even as my father
tore me
and my world
asunder

Therefore
do you wonder
that I was a knife

poised to come down
against my mother's belly
swelling with life

If it was a boy
I'm sorry
except for what he almost certainly would have become

If it was a girl
then I have saved her
from the cruel ripping apart

of the world that should have been
that still might be

if we destroy enough
of what has gone before

Nineteenth-Century Letters

MELVILLE TO HAWTHORNE, 1851

A seeker, not a finder, yet
I swear that I have found in you
Someone to be my friend, my brother—
Come clasp my hand, son of the father
Nor you nor I have ever known,
Come share the seeking. . . .
                                    There are depths
Here under Greylock where I founder,
Sea-wrack tossed up, landlocked and done—
Brother, we die alone. Friend, come!
The hearthfire dies, and no one keeps
Your thoughts as I. Leave your cold light,
Seek in the darkness that we know,
The Godhead broken, we the pieces.

HAWTHORNE TO MELVILLE, 1853

I, who found all evil introspective
In my heart, there found you too—
O restless mariner, persistent quester
After truth, your darker nights
I would have watched with you:
                                    How is it, art
Demands such distances, that we must stand apart?

MELVILLE, RETROSPECTIVE ON HIS WORK, 1891

I quarried the blocks of argument,
Moving them by my skill and sight,
Massive and crude. Of their own weight
In time they settled into place
And broke me. Held in that dark embrace
For years—beneath my monument
To folly, I despaired. But light
Returned, and vision too: Too late,
Perhaps, I saw a distant grace
Break with the dawn upon a face.

Loyalties

Loyalties

Letting Go
Making a World
Portraits
To Give You Words
    Envoi

for the ones who showed me the way

The Covenanters

It seemed I saw them three hundred years from home,
From where their fathers took plain speech and swords
Against the panoply of State and Rome,
Their deeds their only ornament to words.

Their eyes, pale ice in dark impassive faces,
Unsettled the world they looked upon—that gaze,
A heritage from colder northern races
Ungentled by centuries of milder ways.

As in the Puritan portraits, here they stand,
The men the limners saw. And what they see
They set themselves against—their word and hand
Against their times, reckless of history.

Such men are far from home, a destined few,
In any time. Their angry God has hurled
The men who make their conscience what they do
Among us, a type unchanged, to change the world.

For W. B. Yeats, quoting him
"We sing amid our uncertainty"

I sing amid uncertainty,
Certain of this one thing: old man,
You sang beyond the lives of those
You loved, who heard you, left you then,
Impatient with your useless song,
To throw themselves away. And when
You sang among love's leavings, the lot
Of those who live too long, you sang,
"Survive," you sang, "Endure," though that
Was not the meaning of your song.
To win the meaning of the world
From chaos, is uncertain. Bound
To blood and bone, the vision blurs,
The mind cannot prevail, and yet,
Old man, this certainty was yours:
To sing, survives; to sing, endures.

To Sylvia Plath

How tired you must have been,
How cold, that London winter—
Rising at four to write,
Looking for yourself
In that foreign land, your poems
Making friends of strangers,
Strangers of your children,
You, strange to yourself.

Exhausted, chilled, no way
To still the baby's croup,
No way to find four hours'
Unbroken sleep, a marriage
Broken, no way out—
How could you not turn inward
To that one hour where
You knew yourself, perfection
There on the page, taking
No time, no place, to be?

And then the first gray light,
The radiator's bang,
Milk frozen on the sill—
The harsh return. Broken
Again, you must have watched
A stranger feed your children,
Walk to market, join
The literary round.

And did you think that you
Could slip away—no one
To miss you, no one know
Even that you had gone?
You must have thought at last
To fix yourself forever
In the only space
You claimed, to be your poem
Finally, no time, no place.

To a Poet, A. R.

Free, at what cost love might guess—
    you too
        were witness once to goodness

Gassed, jailed, trampled, swept away,
    burnt out
        and broken, bone and nerve,

Yet there you were last night, your voice
    speaking
        your words, the act of language

An act of praise: *stay in the world,*
    keep on,
        you see, it can be done.

Beautiful woman, you stood so straight
    and strong,
        strong at the broken places.

The open heart, spent to exhaustion
    every day,
        is inexhaustible.

at Stanford, March 14, 1975

For Karen

June 27, 1942–June 17, 1976

> Today we are like the children we once were
> Who ran outside when the rain came with the sun,
> Careless in the seemingly endless golden shower
> Until it ceased. And we shivered, and turned to look
> For what we thought would never end, and found
> —The rainbow dimmed, the world grown somehow darker—
> All that treasure gone into the ground.

Letting Go

Changes

for R. G. H.

In laughter, permutation of our tears,
Endurance, of fragility and fears,
And love, created constantly anew,
Now leading, dropping back, and moving through,
Our time is spent in ringing changes, till
Our bells fall silent, and the ropes hang still.

And someone else will toll the passing stroke
To mourn our dead, and tell us to the folk.

Smoke Song

Caught
in the night
and carried

to the light
we cannot see
for chimneys,

hold the dark:
the time we have
we cannot keep;

the day not yet
may never be
for us.

Night Care

for my son

Your comforter, your much-loved bear
Against the grief of future years?
It does not seem enough.
I tuck you in, against a world
Where cold and hurt prevail,
And leave a light against the darkness,
Where in time your way will take you
Where I cannot go.

Dune Fragments

i
Letting go at last
I laughed
Till tears ran down my face.
There are so many ways of giving
Water for a friend.

ii
A smile in this place,
The love
For which we have no words.
Acknowledge here the watermaker,
Water, and our life.

"Love Is the Hardest Lesson"

i
We want. We need.
We learn
that love means bearing
need and want.
We spare each other as we can.
Too often, it is all that we can do.

ii
Knowing what we know
and living as we must,
we hold each other, to make real
the joy of greeting,
or to bear the otherwise unbearable,
the letting go.

Talking to Myself

"You are too indiscriminate
of passion. You have tears
for an onion, fears
for dandelions, (oh
you hide their sun,
to give them
tender loving care)
and probably, somewhere
about you, you have copper pennies
for the eyes of a potato."
What if someday,
I really loved you?
You would never know.